Pure Immanence

Pure Immanence

Essays on A Life

Gilles Deleuze

with an introduction by John Rajchman

Translated by Anne Boyman

ZONE BOOKS · NEW YORK

2005

© 2001 Urzone, Inc.
1226 Prospect Avenue
Brooklyn, NY 11218

First Paperback Edition

"L'Immanence: Une Vie" originally published in *Philosophie* 47
© 1995 Editions de Minuit.

Nietzsche originally published © 1965 PUF

"Hume" originally published in *La Philosophie: De Galilée à
Jean-Jacques Rousseau* © 1972 Hachette.

Printed in the United States of America.

Distributed by The MIT Press,
Cambridge, Massachusetts, and London, England

Library of Congress Cataloging-in-Publication Data

Deleuze, Gilles.
    [Essays. English. Selections]
    Pure immanence: essays on a life / Gilles Deleuze: with an
introduction by John Rajchman; translated by Anne Boyman.
        p.   cm.
    Includes bibliographical references.
    ISBN 1-890951-25-0 (pbk)
    1. Empiricism. 2. Immanence (Philosophy). I. Boyman, Anne.
II. Title.
B2430.D452E54   2001
194—dc21   00-047777
                                                    CIP

Contents

Introduction

John Rajchman

Gilles Deleuze was an empiricist, a logician. That was the source of his lightness, his humor, his naïveté, his practice of philosophy as "a sort of *art brut*" — "I never broke with a kind of empiricism that proceeds to a direct exposition of concepts."[1] It is a shame to present him as a metaphysician and nature mystic. Even in A.N. Whitehead, he admired a "pluralist empiricism" that he found in another way in Michel Foucault — an empiricism of "multiplicities" that says "the abstract doesn't explain, but must itself be explained."[2] Indeed, it was through his logic and his empiricism that Deleuze found his way out of the impasses of the two dominant philosophical schools of his generation, phenomenological and analytic, and elaborated a new conception of sense, neither hermeneutic nor Fregean.[3] He tried to introduce empiricism into his very image of thought, and saw the philosopher as an experimentalist and diagnostician, not as a judge, even of a mystical law.

"…We will speak of a transcendental empiricism in contrast to everything that makes up the world of the subject and the object" he would thus reiterate in the essay that opens this volume. Transcendental empiricism had been Deleuze's way out of the difficulties introduced by Kant and continued in the phenomenological search for an Urdoxa — the difficulties of "transcendental-empirical doubling" and the "traps of consciousness." But what does such empiricism have to do with the two ideas the essay's title joins together — "a life" and "immanence"?

We may think of a life as an empiricist concept in contrast to what John Locke called "the self." [4] A life has quite different features than those Locke associated with the self — consciousness, memory, and personal identity. It unfolds according to another logic: a logic of impersonal individuation rather than personal individualization, of singularities rather than particularities. It can never be completely specified. It is always indefinite — a life. It is only a "virtuality" in the life of the corresponding individual that can sometimes emerge in the strange interval before death. In short, in contrast to the self, a life is "impersonal and yet singular," and so requires a "wilder" sort of empiricism — a transcendental empiricism.

From the start Deleuze sought a conception of empiricism that departs from the classical definition that says that all our ideas can be derived from atomistic sensations through a logic of abstraction and generalization. The real problem of empiricism is rather to be found in a new conception of subjectivity that acquires its full force in Hume, and goes beyond his "associationism" — the problem of a life. A life involves a different "synthesis of the sensible" than the kind that makes possible the conscious self or person. Sensation has a peculiar role in it, and Deleuze talked of a "being of sensation" quite unlike individual sense data waiting to be inserted into a categorical or discursive synthesis providing the unity of their manifold for an "I think." The being of sensation is what can *only* be sensed, since there precisely pre-exists no categorical unity, no *sensus communis* for it. At once more material and less divisible than sense data, it requires a synthesis of another, non-categorical sort, found in artworks, for example. Indeed Deleuze came to think that artworks just *are* sensations connected in materials in such a way as to free *aisthesis* from the assumptions of the sort of "common sense" that for Kant is supposed by the "I think" or the "I judge." Through affect and percept, artworks hit upon something singular yet impersonal in our bodies and brains, irreducible to any pre-existent "we." The "coloring sensations" that Maurice Merleau-Ponty saw in Cézanne are examples of such a spatializing logic of sensation, no longer dominated by classical subject-object relations. But we must push the question of sensation beyond the phenomenological anchoring of a subject in a landscape, for example, in the way Deleuze thinks cinema introduces movement into image, allowing for a distinctive colorism in Jean-Luc Godard.[5] There is still a kind of sensualist piety in Merleau-Ponty — what he called "the flesh" is only the "thermometer of a becoming" given through "asymmetrical syntheses of the sensible" that depart from good form or Gestalt. Such syntheses then require an exercise of thought, which, unlike the syntheses of the self or consciousness, involve a sort of dissolution of the ego. Indeed what Deleuze isolates as "cinema" from the fitful history of filmmaking is in effect nothing other than a multifaceted exploration of this other act of thinking, this other empiricism.

In such cases, sensation is synthesized according to a peculiar logic — a logic of multiplicity that is neither dialectical nor transcendental, prior not simply to the world of subject and object, but also to the logical

connections of subject and predicate and the sets and
functions that Gottlob Frege proposed to substitute
for them. It is a logic of an AND prior and irreducible
to the IS of predications, which Deleuze first finds in
David Hume: "Think *with* AND instead of thinking IS,
instead of thinking *for* IS: empiricism has never had
another secret."[6] It is a constructivist logic of unfin-
ished series rather than a calculus of distinct, count-
able collections; and it is governed by conventions
and problematizations, not axioms and fixed rules of
inference. Its sense is inseparable from play, artifice,
fiction, as, for example, in the case of Lewis Carroll's
"intensive surfaces" for a world that has lost the conventions of its Euclidean skin. Transcendental empiricism may then be said to be the experimental
relation we have to that element in sensation that pre-
cedes the self as well as any "we," through which is
attained, in the materiality of living, the powers of "a
life."

In Stoic logic, Deleuze finds a predecessor for such
a view. But, at the end of the nineteenth century, it is
Henri Bergson and William James who offer us a better philosophical guide to it than do either Husserl or
Frege. Indeed, at one point Deleuze remarks that the
very idea of a "plane of immanence" requires a kind
of "radical empiricism" — an empiricism whose force

11

"…begins from the moment it defines the subject: a habitus, a habit, nothing more than a habit in a field of immanence, the habit of saying I."[7] Among the classical empiricists, it is Hume who poses such questions, Hume who redirects the problem of empiricism toward the new questions that would be elaborated by Bergson and Nietzsche.

That is the subject of Deleuze's youthful *Memoire*. He sees Hume as connecting empiricism and subjectivity in a new way, departing from Locke on the question of personal identity. In Locke's conception, the self is neither what the French call *le moi* or *le je* — the I or the me.[8] Rather it is defined by individual "ownership" (*my*self, *your*self) and sameness over time (identity). Locke thus introduces the problem of identity and diversity into our philosophical conception of ourselves. What the young Deleuze found singular in Hume's empiricism is then the idea that this self, this person, this possession, is in fact not *given*. Indeed the self is only a fiction or artifice in which, through habit, we come to believe, a sort of incorrigible illusion of living; and it is as this artifice that the self becomes fully part of nature — *our* nature. Hume thus opens up the question of other ways of composing sensations than those of the habits of the self and the "human nature" that they suppose. A new or "superior empiri-

12

cism" becomes possible, one concerned with what is singular yet "in-human" in the composition of ourselves. Deleuze would find it in Bergson and Nietzsche, who imagined a "free difference" in living, un-conscious and no longer enclosed within a personal identity.

While Deleuze shared with his French contemporaries a suspicion about a constituting subject or consciousness, in Hume he found a new empiricist way out of it, which he urged against phenomenology and its tendency to reintroduce a transcendental ego or a material a priori. The real problem dramatized in Hume's humorous picture of the self as incorrigible illusion is how our lives ever acquire the consistency of an enduring self, given that it is born of "... delirium, chance, indifference"[9]; and the question then is: can we construct an empiricist or experimental relation to the persistence of this zone or plane of pre-subjective delirium and pre-individual singularity in our lives and in our relations with others?

Immanence and a life thus suppose one another. For immanence is pure only when it is not immanent *to* a prior subject or object, mind or matter, only when, neither innate nor acquired, it is always yet "in the making"; and "a life" is a potential or virtuality subsisting in just such a purely immanent plane. Unlike *the* life of an individual, *a* life is thus necessarily vague or indefinite, and this indefiniteness is real. It is vague in the Peircian sense that the real is itself indeterminate or anexact, beyond the limitations of our capacities to measure it. We thus each have the pre-predicative vagueness of Adam in Paradise that Leibniz envisaged in his letters to Arnauld.[10] We are always *quelconque* — we are and remain "anybodies" before we become "somebodies." Underneath the identity of our bodies or organisms, we each have what Deleuze calls *a* body (*a* mouth, *a* stomach, etc). We thus have the singularity of what Spinoza already termed "a singular essence," and of what makes the Freudian unconscious singular, each of us possessed of a peculiar "complex" unfolding through the time of our lives. How then can we make such pre-individual singularities coincide in space and time; and what is the space and time that includes them?

We need a new conception of society in which what we have in common is our singularities and not our individualities — where what is common is "impersonal" and what is "impersonal" is common. That is precisely what Charles Dickens's tale shows — only through a process of "im-personalization" in the interval between life and death does the hero become our "common friend." It is also what Deleuze brings out in Hume: the new questions of empiricism and subjectivity discover their full force only in Hume's social thought. In the place of the dominant idea of a social contract among already given selves or subjects, Hume elaborates an original picture of convention that allows for an "attunement" of the passions prior to the identities of reason; only in this way can we escape the violence toward others inherent in the formation of our social identities or the problem of our "partialities." Hume thus prepares the way for a view of society not as contract but as experiment — experiment with what in life is prior to both possessive individuals and traditional social wholes. Property, for example, becomes nothing more than an evolving jurisprudential convention.

There is, in short, an element in experience that comes before the determination of subject and sense. Shown through a "diagram" that one constructs to move about more freely rather than a space defined by an a priori "scheme" into which one inserts oneself, it involves a temporality that is always starting up again in the midst, and relations with others based not in identification or recognition, but encounter and new compositions. In *Difference and Repetition*, Deleuze tries to show that what characterizes the "modern work" is not self-reference but precisely the attempt to introduce such difference into the very idea of sensation, discovering syntheses prior to the identities of figure and perception — a sort of great laboratory for a higher empiricism. Of this experience or experiment, Nietzsche's Ariadne figures as the dramatic heroine or conceptual persona: "... (Ariadne has hung herself). The work of art leaves the domain of representation to become 'experience,' transcendental empiricism or science of the sensible..."[11]

But to assume this role Ariadne must herself undergo a transformation, a "becoming." She must hang herself with the famous thread her father gave her to help the hero Theseus escape from the labyrinth. For tied up with the thread, she remains a "cold creature of resentment." Such is her mystery — the key to Deleuze's subtle view of Nietzsche. The force of her femininity is thus unlike that of Antigone, who preserves her identification with her dead father, Oedipus, through a defiant "pure negation" that can no longer be reabsorbed in Creon's city. Ariadne becomes the heroine who says "yes" rather than "no" — yes to what is "outside" our given determinations or identities. She becomes a heroine not of mourning but of the breath and plasticity of life, of dance and lightness — of the light Earth of which Zarathustra says that it must be approached in many ways, since *the* way does not exist. She thus points to an empiricist way out of the impasses of nihilism.

16

For the problem with Theseus becoming a German, all-too-German hero is that even if God is dead, one still believes in "the subject," "the individual," "human nature." Abandoned by Theseus, approaching Dionysius, Ariadne introduces instead a belief in the world and in the potentials of a life. We thus arrive at an original view of the problem of nihilism in Nietzsche as that partially physiological condition in which such belief in the world is lost. In fact it is a problem that goes back to Hume. For it is Hume who substitutes for the Cartesian problem of certainty and doubt, the new questions of belief and probable inference. To think is not to be certain, but, on the contrary, to believe where we cannot know for sure. In his *Dialogues on Natural Religion* (which Deleuze counts as the only genuine dialogue in the history of philosophy), Hume suggests that God as well as the self be regarded as a fiction required by our nature. The problem of religion is then no longer whether God exists, but whether we need the idea of God in order to exist, or, in the terms of Pascal's wager, who has the better mode of existence, the believer or the nonbeliever. It is here that Deleuze thinks Nietzsche goes beyond Hume, who, in connecting belief and probability, found the idea of chance to be quite meaningless.[12] By contrast, Nietzsche introduces a conception of chance as distinct from probability into the very experience of thought and the way the "game of thought" is played (its rules, its players, its aims). He asks what it means to think that the world is always making itself while God is calculating, such that his calculations never come out right; and so he extends the question of belief to the plane of "delirium, chance, indifference" out of which the habits of self are formed and from which the potentials of a life take off. Nihilism is then the state in which the belief in the potentials of a life, and so of chance and disparity in the world, has been lost. Conversely, as Ariadne becomes light, what she affirms is that to think is not to be certain nor yet to calculate probabilities. It is to say yes to what is singular yet impersonal in living; and for that one must believe in the world and not in the fictions of God or the self that Hume thought derived from it.

Deleuze calls this way out of nihilism an "empiricist conversion," and in his last writing, it gains a peculiar urgency. "Yes, the problem has changed" he declares in *What is Philosophy?* "It may be that to believe in this world, in this life, has become our most difficult task, the task of a mode of existence to be discovered on our plane of immanence today."[13] Although the three essays in this volume each take up

18

this question, they in fact come from different junctures in Deleuze's journey. The essays on Hume and Nietzsche are from a first phase, after World War II, when Deleuze tried to extract a new image of thought from the many different strata of the philosophical tradition, and so rethink the relation of thought to life; the image of a "superior empiricism" accompanies all these attempts. The first or lead essay, however, was Deleuze's last. It comes from a late phase of "clinical" essays, in which Deleuze takes up again the many paths and trajectories composing his work, some leading to "impasses closed off by illness."[14] Vital, often humorous, these essays are short, abrupt in their transitions and endings. They have something of Franz Kafka's parables or the aphorisms Nietzsche likened to shouting from one Alpine peak to another — one must condense and distill one's message, as with Adorno's image, invoked by Deleuze, of a bottle thrown into the sea of communication. For it is in the idea of communication that Deleuze came to think philosophy confronts a new and most insolent rival. Indeed that is just why the problem has changed, calling for a fresh "empiricist conversion" and a *Kunstwollen* or a "becoming-art" of the sort he imagined the art of cinema had offered us in the rather different circumstances of uncertainty following World War II.[15]

Written in a strange interval before his own death, "Immanence ... a life" has been regarded as a kind of testament. What is clear is that Deleuze took its "last message" to occur at a time of renewed difficulty and possibility for philosophy. As with Bergson, one needed to again introduce movement into thought rather than trying to find universals of information or communication — in particular into the very image of the brain and contemporary neuroscience. In the place of artificial intelligence, one needed to construct a new picture of the brain as a "relatively undifferentiated matter" into which thinking and art might introduce new connections that didn't preexist them — as it were, the brain as materiality of "a life" yet to be invented, prior and irreducible to consciousness as well as machines. In his last writing, "Immanence ... a life," we sense not only this new problem and this new urgency, but also the force of the long, incredible voyage in which Deleuze kept alive the singular image of thought which has the naïveté and the strength to believe that "philosophy brings about a vast deviation of wisdom — it puts it in the service of a pure immanence."[16]

NOTES

1. *Pourparlers* (Paris: Minuit, 1990), p. 122.

2. *Dialogues* (New York: Columbia University Press, 1987), p. vii, following the declaration "I have always felt that I am an empiricist, that is, a pluralist."

3. Claude Imbert examines "why and how an empiricist philosopher, as Deleuze certainly was, became all the more interested in logic" (Unpublished MS). Her *Pour une histoire de la logique* (Paris: PUF, 1999) may be read as an attempt to imagine what a history of logic might look like from this peculiar empiricist point of view; it thus expands on her earlier work *Phenome-nologies et langues formulaires* (Paris: PUF, 1992), in which she closely examines the internal difficulties in the phenomenological and analytic traditions leading to the late Merleau-Ponty and Wittgenstein. In this way, Imbert offers a more promising approach to the problem of the relation of Deleuzian multiplicity to set theory than does Alain Badiou in his odd attempt to recast it along Lacanian lines.

4. Etienne Balibar makes a detailed case for Locke rather than Descartes as the inventor of the philosophical concept of consciousness and the self. See his introduction to John Locke, *Identité et différence* (Paris: Seuil, 1998).

5. See *L'Image-mouvement* (Paris: Minuit, 1983), pp. 83ff. for Deleuze's account of why Bergson offers a "cinematic" way out of the crisis in psychology in the nineteenth century that contrasts with Husserl and the subsequent focus on painting in

21

phenomenology. In his *Suspensions of Perception* (Cambridge, MA: MIT Press, 1999), Jonathan Crary goes on to show how this analysis may be extended to painting. In the late Cézanne, he finds a more Bergsonian synthesis, as yet unavailable to Manet or Seurat, a "...rhythmic coexistence of radically heterogeneous and temporally dispersed elements," which "...instead of holding together the contents of the perceived world, seeks to enter into its ceaseless movements of destabilization" (p. 297).

6. *Dialogues*, p. 57.

7. *Qu'est-ce que la philosophie?* (Paris: Minuit, 1977), p. 49.

8. Paul Patton translates *le je* and *le moi*, of which it is question throughout *Difference and Repetition,* as "the I" and "the self." Strictly speaking, however, the self is *le soi*, which, according to Etienne Balibar, in fact comes into philosophical French via Locke, its inventor. Balibar tries to sort out the philosophical implications of such terminological differences in his entry "Je/moi/soi" for *Vocabulaire européen des philosophies* (Paris: Seuil, 2001). He sees the problem of the I and the Me as deriving from a Kantian recasting of Descartes's cogito, while the Lockean self starts another minor tradition that leads past Kant to James and Bergson.

9. *Empirisme et subjectivité* (Paris: PUF, 1953), p. 4.

10. See *Logique du sens* (Paris: Minuit, 1969), pp. 138ff. The problem of "vague Adam" is then put in these terms: "...the individual is always *quelconque* (anyone), born like Eve from a

22

side of Adam, from a singularity…out of a pre-individual transcendental field," (pp. 141–42).

11. *Différence et répétition* (Paris: PUF, 1968), p. 79.

12. On the contrast between Hume and both Peirce and Nietzsche on this score see Ian Hacking, *The Taming of Chance* (New York: Cambridge University Press, 1990). Hacking's "untamed" chance is akin to the "nomadic" chance that Deleuze discusses, for example, in *Différence et répétition*, pp. 361ff. in terms of the transformations of the game of thought.

13. *Qu'est-ce que la philosophie?*, pp. 72–73.

14. *Critique et clinique* (Paris: Minuit, 1993), p. 10.

15. See *L'image-temps* (Paris: Minuit, 1985), pp. 223ff. "Only belief in the world can reconnect man to what he sees and hears … to give us back belief in the world — such is the power of modern cinema…."

16. *Qu'est-ce que la philosophie?*, p. 46.

CHAPTER ONE

Immanence: A Life

What is a transcendental field? It can be distinguished from experience in that it doesn't refer to an object or belong to a subject (empirical representation). It appears therefore as a pure stream of a-subjective consciousness, a pre-reflexive impersonal consciousness, a qualitative duration of consciousness without a self. It may seem curious that the transcendental be defined by such immediate givens: we will speak of a transcendental empiricism in contrast to everything that makes up the world of the subject and the object. There is something wild and powerful in this transcendental empiricism that is of course not the element of sensation (simple empiricism), for sensation is only a break within the flow of absolute consciousness. It is, rather, however close two sensations may be, the passage from one to the other as becoming, as increase or decrease in power (virtual quantity). Must

we then define the transcendental field by a pure immediate consciousness with neither object nor self,
as a movement that neither begins nor ends? (Even
Spinoza's conception of this passage or quantity of
power still appeals to consciousness.)

But the relation of the transcendental field to consciousness is only a conceptual one. Consciousness
becomes a fact only when a subject is produced at the
same time as its object, both being outside the field
and appearing as "transcendents." Conversely, as long
as consciousness traverses the transcendental field at
an infinite speed everywhere diffused, nothing is able
to reveal it.[1] It is expressed, in fact, only when it is
reflected on a subject that refers it to objects. That is
why the transcendental field cannot be defined by the
consciousness that is coextensive with it, but removed
from any revelation.

The transcendent is not the transcendental. Were it
not for consciousness, the transcendental field would
be defined as a pure plane of immanence, because it
eludes all transcendence of the subject and of the
object.[2] Absolute immanence is in itself: it is not in
something, *to* something; it does not depend on an
object or belong to a subject. In Spinoza, immanence
is not immanence *to* substance; rather, substance and
modes are in immanence. When the subject or the

object falling outside the plane of immanence is taken as a universal subject or as any object *to which* immanence is attributed, the transcendental is entirely denatured, for it then simply redoubles the empirical (as with Kant), and immanence is distorted, for it then finds itself enclosed in the transcendent. Immanence is not related to Some Thing as a unity superior to all things or to a Subject as an act that brings about a synthesis of things: it is only when immanence is no longer immanence to anything other than itself that we can speak of a plane of immanence. No more than the transcendental field is defined by consciousness can the plane of immanence be defined by a subject or an object that is able to contain it.

We will say of pure immanence that it is A LIFE, and nothing else. It is not immanence to life, but the immanent that is in nothing is itself a life. A life is the immanence of immanence, absolute immanence: it is complete power, complete bliss. It is to the degree that he goes beyond the aporias of the subject and the object that Johann Fichte, in his last philosophy, presents the transcendental field as *a life*, no longer dependent on a Being or submitted to an Act — it is an absolute immediate consciousness whose very activity no longer refers to a being but is ceaselessly posed in a life.[3] The transcendental field then becomes a genuine plane of immanence that reintroduces Spinozism into the heart of the philosophical process. Did Maine de Biran not go through something similar in his "last philosophy" (the one he was too tired to bring to fruition) when he discovered, beneath the transcendence of effort, an absolute immanent life? The transcendental field is defined by a plane of immanence, and the plane of immanence by a life.

What is immanence? A life... No one has described what *a* life is better than Charles Dickens, if we take the indefinite article as an index of the transcendental. A disreputable man, a rogue, held in contempt by everyone, is found as he lies dying. Suddenly, those taking care of him manifest an eagerness, respect, even love, for his slightest sign of life. Everybody bustles about to save him, to the point where, in his deepest coma, this wicked man himself senses something soft and sweet penetrating him. But to the degree that he comes back to life, his saviors turn colder, and he becomes once again mean and crude. Between his life and his death, there is a moment that is only that of *a* life playing with death.[4] The life of the individual gives way to an impersonal and yet singular life that releases a pure event freed from the accidents of internal and external life, that is, from the subjectivity and objectivity of what happens: a "Homo tantum" with whom everyone empathizes and who attains a sort of beatitude. It is a haecceity no longer of individuation but of singularization: a life of pure immanence, neutral, beyond good and evil, for it was only the subject that incarnated it in the midst of things that made it good or bad. The life of such individuality fades away in favor of the singular life immanent to a man who no longer has a name, though he can be mistaken for no other. A singular essence, a life...

But we shouldn't enclose life in the single moment when individual life confronts universal death. *A* life is everywhere, in all the moments that a given living subject goes through and that are measured by given lived objects: an immanent life carrying with it the events or singularities that are merely actualized in subjects and objects. This indefinite life does not itself have moments, close as they may be one to another, but only between-times, between-moments; it doesn't just come about or come after but offers the immensity of an empty time where one sees the event yet to come and already happened, in the absolute of an immediate consciousness. In his novels, Alexander Lernet-Holenia places the event in an in-between time that could engulf entire armies. The singularities and the events that constitute *a* life coexist with the accidents of *the* life that corresponds to it, but they

29

are neither grouped nor divided in the same way. They connect with one another in a manner entirely differ-ent from how individuals connect. It even seems that a singular life might do without any individuality, without any other concomitant that individualizes it. For example, very small children all resemble one another and have hardly any individuality, but they have singularities: a smile, a gesture, a funny face — not subjective qualities. Small children, through all their sufferings and weaknesses, are infused with an immanent life that is pure power and even bliss. The indefinite aspects in a life lose all indetermination to the degree that they fill out a plane of immanence or, what amounts to the same thing, to the degree that they constitute the elements of a transcendental field (in-dividual life, on the other hand, remains inseparable from empirical determinations). The indefinite as such is the mark not of an empirical indetermination but of a determination by immanence or a transcendental determinability. The indefinite article is the indeter-mination of the person only because it is determina-tion of the singular. The One is not the transcendent that might contain immanence but the immanent con-tained within a transcendental field. One is always the index of a multiplicity: an event, a singularity, a life... Although it is always possible to invoke a transcendent that falls outside the plane of immanence, or that attributes immanence to itself, all transcendence is constituted solely in the flow of immanent consciousness that belongs to this plane.[5] Transcendence is always a product of immanence.

A life contains only virtuals. It is made up of virtualities, events, singularities. What we call virtual is not something that lacks reality but something that is engaged in a process of actualization following the plane that gives it its particular reality. The immanent event is actualized in a state of things and of the lived that make it happen. The plane of immanence is itself actualized in an object and a subject to which it attributes itself. But however inseparable an object and a subject may be from their actualization, the plane of immanence is itself virtual, so long as the events that populate it are virtualities. Events or singularities give to the plane all their virtuality, just as the plane of immanence gives virtual events their full reality. The event considered as non-actualized (indefinite) is lacking in nothing. It suffices to put it in relation to its concomitants: a transcendental field, a plane of immanence, a life, singularities. A wound is incarnated or actualized in a state of things or of life; but it is itself a pure virtuality on the plane of immanence that leads us into a life. My wound existed before me: not

31

a transcendence of the wound as higher actuality, but its immanence as a virtuality always within a milieu (plane or field).[6] There is a big difference between the virtuals that define the immanence of the transcendental field and the possible forms that actualize them and transform them into something transcendent.

NOTES

1. "As though we reflected back to surfaces the light which emanates from them, the light which, had it passed unopposed, would never have been revealed" (Henri Bergson, *Matter and Memory* [New York: Zone Books, 1988], p. 36).

2. Cf. Jean-Paul Sartre, who posits a transcendental field without a subject that refers to a consciousness that is impersonal, absolute, immanent: with respect to it, the subject and the object are "transcendents" (*La transcendance de l'Ego* [Paris: Vrin, 1966], pp. 74–87). On James, see David Lapoujade's analysis, "Le Flux intensif de la conscience chez William James," *Philosophie* 46 (June 1995).

3. Already in the second introduction to *La Doctrine de la science*: "The intuition of pure activity which is nothing fixed, but progress, not a being, but a life" (*Oeuvres choisies de la philosophie première* [Paris: Vrin, 1964], p. 274). On the concept of life according to Fichte, see *Initiation à la vie bienheureuse* (Paris: Aubier, 1944), and Martial Guéroult's commentary (p. 9).

4. Dickens, *Our Mutual Friend* (New York: Oxford University Press, 1989), p. 443.

5. Even Edmund Husserl admits this: "The being of the world is necessarily transcendent to consciousness, even within the originary evidence, and remains necessarily transcendent to it. But this doesn't change the fact that all transcendence is constituted solely in the *life of consciousness*, as inseparably linked to that life…" (*Méditations cartésiennes* [Paris: Vrin, 1947], p. 52). This will be the starting point of Sartre's text.

6. Cf. Joë Bousquet, *Les Capitales* (Paris: Le Cercle du Livre, 1955).

Chapter Two

Hume

The Meaning of Empiricism

The history of philosophy has more or less absorbed, more or less digested, empiricism. It has defined empiricism as the reverse of rationalism: Is there or is there not in ideas something that is not in the senses or the sensible? It has made of empiricism a critique of innateness, of the *a priori*. But empiricism has always harbored other secrets. And it is they that David Hume pushes the furthest and fully illuminates in his extremely difficult and subtle work. Hume's position is therefore quite peculiar. His empiricism is a sort of science-fiction universe *avant la lettre*. As in science fiction, one has the impression of a fictive, foreign world, seen by other creatures, but also the presentiment that this world is already ours, and those creatures, ourselves. A parallel conversion of science or theory follows: theory becomes an *inquiry* (the origin of this conception is in Francis Bacon; Immanuel Kant will recall it while transforming and rationalising it when he conceives of theory as a court or tribunal). Science or theory is an inquiry, which is to say, a practice: a practice of the seemingly fictive world that empiricism describes; a study of the conditions of legitimacy of practices in this empirical world that is in fact our own. The result is a great conversion of theory to practice. The manuals of the history of philosophy misunderstand what they call "associationism" when they see it as a theory in the ordinary sense of the term and as an inverted rationalism. Hume raises unexpected questions that seem nevertheless familiar: To establish possession of an abandoned city, does a javelin thrown against the door suffice, or must the door be touched by a finger? To what extent can we be owners of the seas? Why is the ground more important than the surface in a juridical system, whereas in painting, the paint is more important than the canvas? It is only then that the problem of the association of ideas discovers its meaning. What is called the theory of association finds its direction and its truth in a casuistry of relations, a practice of law, of politics, of economics, that completely changes the nature of philosophical reflection.

The Nature of Relations

Hume's originality — or one of Hume's originalities — comes from the force with which he asserts that *relations are external to their terms*. We can understand such a thesis only in contrast to the entire endeavor of philosophy as rationalism and its attempt to reduce the paradox of relations: either by finding a way of making relations internal to their own terms or by finding a deeper and more comprehensive term to which the relation would itself be internal. "Peter is smaller than Paul": How can we make of this relation something internal to Peter, or to Paul, or to their concept, or to the whole they form, or to the Idea in which they participate? How can we overcome the irreducible exteriority of relations? Empiricism had always fought for the exteriority of relations. But in a certain way, its position on this remained obscured by the problem of the origin of knowledge or of ideas, according to which everything finds its origin in the sensible and in the operations of the mind upon the sensible.

Hume effects an inversion that would take empiricism to a higher power: if ideas contain nothing other and nothing more than what is contained in sensory impressions, it is precisely because relations are external and heterogeneous to their terms — impressions

37

or ideas. Thus the difference isn't between ideas *and* impressions but between two sorts of impressions or ideas: impressions or ideas of terms *and* impressions or ideas of relations. The real empiricist world is thereby laid out for the first time to the fullest: it is a world of exteriority, a world in which thought itself exists in a fundamental relationship with the Outside, a world in which terms are veritable atoms and relations veritable external passages; a world in which the conjunction "and" dethrones the interiority of the verb "is"; a harlequin world of multicolored patterns and non-totalizable fragments where communication takes place through external relations. Hume's thought is built up in a double way: through the *atomism* that shows how ideas or sensory impressions refer to punctual minima producing time and space; and through the *associationism* that shows how relations are established between these terms, always external to them, and dependent on other principles. On the one hand, a physics of the mind; on the other, a logic of relations. It is thus Hume who first breaks with the constraining form of predicative judgment and makes possible an autonomous logic of relations, discovering a conjunctive world of atoms and relations, later developed by Bertrand Russell and modern logic, for relations are the conjunctions themselves.

38

Human Nature

What is a relation? It is what makes us pass from a given impression or idea to the idea of something that is not presently given. For example, I think of something "similar"... When I see a picture of Peter, I think of Peter, who isn't there. One would look in vain in the given term for the reason for this passage. The relation is itself the effect of so-called principles of association, contiguity, resemblance, and causality, all of which constitute, precisely, a *human nature*. Human nature means that what is universal or constant in the human mind is never one idea or another as a term but only the ways of passing from one particular idea to another. Hume, in this sense, will devote himself to a concerted destruction of the three great terminal ideas of metaphysics: the Self, the World, and God. And yet at first Hume's thesis seems disappointing: what is the advantage of explaining relations by principles of human nature, which are principles of association that seem just another way of designating relations? But this disappointment derives from a misunderstanding of the problem, for the problem is not of causes but of the way relations function as effects of those causes and the practical conditions of this functioning.

Let us consider in this regard a very special relation:

causality. It is special because it doesn't simply go from a given term to the idea of something that isn't presently given. Causality requires that I go from something that is given to me to the idea of something that has never been given to me, that isn't even giveable in experience. For example, based on some signs in a book, I believe that Caesar lived. When I see the sun rise, I say that it will rise tomorrow; having seen water boil at 100 degrees, I say that it necessarily boils at 100 degrees. Yet expressions such as "tomorrow," "always," "necessarily," convey something that cannot be given in experience: tomorrow isn't given without becoming today, without ceasing to be tomorrow, and all experience is experience of a contingent particular. In other words, causality is a relation according to which I go beyond the given; I say more than what is given or giveable — in short, *I infer and I believe*, I expect that... This, Hume's first displacement, is crucial, for it puts belief at the basis and the origin of knowledge. The functioning of causal relations can then be explained as follows: as similar cases are observed (all the times I have seen that *a* follows or accompanies *b*), they fuse in the imagination, while remaining distinct and separate from each other in our understanding. This property of fusion in the imagination constitutes habit (I expect...), at the same time as distinction in the understanding tailors belief to the calculus of observed cases (probability as calculus of degrees of belief). The principle of habit as fusion of similar cases in the imagination and the principle of experience as observation of distinct cases in the understanding thus combine to produce both the relation and the inference that follows from the relation (belief), through which causality functions.

Fiction

Fiction and Nature are arranged in a particular way in the empiricist world. Left to itself, the mind has the capacity to move from one idea to another, but it does so at random, in a delirium that runs throughout the universe, creating fire dragons, winged horses, and monstrous giants. The principles of human nature, on the other hand, impose constant rules on this delirium: laws of passage, of transition, of inference, which are in accordance with Nature itself. But then a strange battle takes place, for if it is true that the principles of association shape the mind, by imposing on it a nature that disciplines the delirium or the fictions of the imagination, conversely, the imagination uses these same principles to make its fictions or its fantasies acceptable and to give them a warrant they wouldn't have on their own. In this sense, it belongs to fiction to feign these relations, to induce fictive ones, and to make us believe in our follies. We see this not only in the gift fantasy has of doubling any present relation with other relations that don't exist in a given case. But especially in the case of causality, fantasy forges fictive causal chains, illegitimate rules, simulacra of belief, either by conflating the accidental and the essential or by using the properties of language (going beyond experience) to substitute for the repetition of similar cases actually observed a simple verbal repetition that only simulates its effect. It is thus that the liar believes in his lies by dint of repeating them; education, superstition, eloquence, and poetry also work in this way. One no longer goes beyond experience in a scientific way that will be confirmed by Nature itself and by a corresponding calculus; one goes beyond it in all the directions of a delirium that forms a counter-Nature, allowing for the fusion of anything at all. Fantasy uses the principles of association to turn them around, giving them an illegitimate extension. Hume thereby effects a second great displacement in philosophy, which consists in substituting for the traditional concept of error a concept of delirium or illusion, according to which there are beliefs that are not false but illegitimate — illegitimate exercises of faculties, illegitimate functioning of relations. In this as well, Kant owes something essential to Hume: we are not threatened by error, rather and much worse, we bathe in delirium.

But this would still be nothing as long as the fictions of fantasy turn the principles of human nature against themselves in conditions that can always be corrected, as, for example, in the case of causality, where a strict calculus of probabilities can denounce delirious extrapolations or feigned relations. But the illusion is considerably worse when it belongs to human nature, in other words, when the illegitimate exercise or belief is incorrigible, inseparable from legitimate beliefs, and indispensable to their organization. In this case, the fanciful usage of the principles of human nature itself becomes a principle. Fiction and delirium shift over to the side of human nature. That is what Hume will show in his most subtle, most difficult, analyses concerning the Self, the World, and God: how the positing of the existence of distinct and continuous bodies, how the positing of an identity of the self, requires the intervention of all sorts of fictive uses of relations, and in particular of causality, in conditions where no fiction can be corrected but where each instead plunges us into other fictions, which all form part of human nature. In a posthumous work that is perhaps his masterpiece, *Dialogues Concerning Natural Religion*, Hume goes on to apply the same critical method not simply to revealed religions but also to so-called natural religion and to the teleological arguments on which it is based. Here, Hume is at his most humorous: beliefs, he says, all the more form part of our nature as they are completely illegitimate from the point of view of the principles of human nature. It is no doubt in this way that we should understand the complex notion of *modern skepticism* developed by Hume. Unlike ancient skepticism, which was based on the variety of sensible appearances and errors of sense, modern skepticism is based on the status of relations and their exteriority. The first act of modern skepticism consisted in making belief the basis of knowledge — in other words, in naturalizing belief (positivism). The second act consisted in denouncing illegitimate beliefs as those which don't obey the rules that are in fact productive of knowledge (probabilism, calculus of probabilities). But in a final refinement, or third act, illegitimate beliefs in the Self, the World, and God appear as the horizon of all possible legitimate beliefs, or as the lowest degree of belief. For if everything is belief, including knowledge, everything is a question of degree of belief, even the delirium of non-knowledge. Humor, the modern skeptical virtue of Hume, against irony, the ancient dogmatic virtue of Plato and Socrates.

The Imagination

If the inquiry into knowledge has skepticism as its principle and its outcome, if it leads to an inextricable mix of fiction and human nature, it is perhaps because it is only one part of the inquiry, and not even the main one. The principles of association in fact acquire their sense only in relation to passions: not only do affective circumstances guide the associations of ideas, but the relations themselves are given a meaning, a direction, an irreversibility, an exclusivity as a result of the passions. In short, what constitutes human nature, what gives the mind a nature or a constancy, is not only the principles of association from which relations derive but also the principles of passion from which "inclinations" follow. Two things must be kept in mind in this regard: that the passions don't shape the mind or give it a nature in the same way as do the principles of association; and that, on the other hand, the source of the mind as delirium or fiction doesn't react to the passions in the same way as it does to relations.

We have seen how the principles of association, and especially causality, required the mind to go beyond the given, inspiring in it beliefs or extrapolations not all of which were illegitimate. But the passions have the effect of restricting the range of the mind, fixating it on privileged ideas and objects, for the basis of passion is not egotism but *partiality*, which is much worse. We are passionate in the first place about our parents, about those who are close to us and are like us (restricted causality, contiguity, resemblance). This is worse than being governed by egotism, for our egotisms would only have to be curtailed for society to become possible. From the sixteenth to the eighteenth century, the famous theories of contract posed the problem of society in such terms: a limitation, or even a renunciation, of natural rights, from which a contractual society might be born. But we should not see Hume's saying that man is by nature partial rather than egotistical as a simple nuance; rather, we should see it as a radical change in the practical way the problem of society is posed. The problem is no longer how to limit egotisms and the corresponding natural rights but how to go beyond partialities, how to pass from a "limited sympathy" to an "extended generosity," how to stretch passions and give them an extension they don't have on their own. Society is thus seen no longer as a system of legal and contractual limitations but as an institutional invention: how can we *invent artifices*, how can we create institutions that force passions to go beyond their partialities and form moral, judicial, political sentiments (for example, the feeling of justice)? There follows the opposition Hume sets up between contract and convention or artifice. Hume is probably the first to have broken with the limiting model of contract and law that dominated the sociology of the eighteenth century and to oppose to it a positive model of artifice and institution. Thus the entire question of man is displaced in turn: it is no longer, as with knowledge, a matter of the complex relation between fiction and human nature; it is, rather, a matter of the relation between human nature and artifice (man as inventive species).

The Passions

We have seen that with knowledge the principles of human nature instituted rules of extension or extrapolation that fantasy in turn used to make acceptable simulacra of belief, such that a calculus was always necessary to correct, to select the legitimate from the illegitimate. With passion, on the other hand, the problem is posed differently: how can we invent an artificial extension that goes beyond the partiality of human nature? Here fantasy or fiction takes on a new

47

meaning. As Hume says, the mind and its fantasies
behave with respect to passions not in the manner of
a wind instrument but in the manner of a percussive
instrument, "where, after each beat, the vibrations
still retain some sound which gradually and imper-
ceptibly dies." In short, it is up to the imagination to
reflect passion, to make it resonate and go beyond the
limits of its natural partiality and presentness. Hume
shows how aesthetic and moral sentiments are formed
in this way: the passions reflected in the imagination
become themselves imaginary. In reflecting the passions, the imagination liberates them, stretching them
out infinitely and projecting them beyond their natural limits. Yet on at least one count, we must correct
the metaphor of percussion: as they resonate in the
imagination, the passions do not simply become gradually less vivid and less present; they also change their
color or sound, as when the sadness of a passion represented in a tragedy turns into the pleasure of an
almost infinite play of the imagination; they assume a
new nature and are accompanied by a new kind of
belief. Thus the will "moves easily in all directions
and produces an image of itself, even in places where
it is not fixed."

This is what makes up the world of artifice or of
culture: this resonance, this reflexion of the passions

in the imagination, which makes of culture at once
the most frivolous and the most serious thing. But
how can we avoid two deficiencies in these cultural
formations? On the one hand, how to avoid the enlarged passions being less vivid than the present ones,
even if they have a different nature, and, on the other,
how to avoid their becoming completely undeter-
mined, projecting their weakened images in all directions independently of any rule. The first problem is
resolved through agencies of social power sanctions
or the techniques of rewards and punishments, which
confer on the enlarged sentiments or reflected passions an added degree of vividness or belief: princi-
pally government, but also more subterranean and
implicit agencies, like custom and taste. In this regard, too, Hume is the first to have posed the problem
of power and government in terms not of representa-
tivity but of credibility.

The second point is also relevant to the way in
which Hume's philosophy forms a general system. If
the passions are reflected in the imagination or in fantasy, it is not an imagination that is naked but one that
has already been fixed or naturalized by the principles
of association. Resemblance, contiguity, causality — in
short, all the relations that are the object of a knowledge or a calculus, that provide general rules for the

determination of reflected sentiments beyond the immediate and restricted way in which they are used by non-reflected passions. Thus aesthetic sentiments find in the principles of association veritable rules of taste. Hume also shows in detail how, by being reflected in the imagination, the passion of possession discovers in the principles of association the means to determine the general rules that constitute the factors of property or the world of law. A whole study of the variations of relations, a whole calculus of relations, is involved, which allows one to respond in each case to the question: Does there exist, between a given person and a given object, a relation of a nature such as to have us believe (or our imagination believe) in an appropriation of one by the other. "A man who has chased a hare to the point of exhaustion would consider it an injustice if another person pushed ahead of him and seized his prey. But the same man who goes to pick an apple that hangs within his reach has no reason to complain if another man, quicker than he, reaches beyond him and takes it for himself. What is the reason for this difference if not the fact that immobility, which is not natural to the hare, is closely related to the hunter, whereas this relation is lacking in the other case?" Does the throw of a javelin against a door ensure the ownership of an abandoned city, or must a finger touch the door in order to establish a sufficient relation? Why, according to civil law, does the ground win out over the surface, but paint over the canvas, whereas paper wins out over writing? The principles of association find their true sense in a casuistry of relations that works out the details of the worlds of culture and of law. And this is the true object of Hume's philosophy: relations as the means of an activity and a practice — juridical, economic and political.

A Popular and Scientific Philosophy

Hume was a particularly precocious philosopher: at around twenty-five years old, he wrote his important book *A Treatise of Human Nature* (published in 1739–1740). A new tone in philosophy, an extraordinary firmness and simplicity emerge from a great complexity of arguments, which bring into play the exercise of fictions, the science of human nature, and the practice of artifice. A philosophy at once popular and scientific — a sort of pop philosophy, which for its ideal had a decisive clarity, a clarity not of ideas but of relations and operations. It was this clarity that Hume would try to impose in his subsequent works, even if this meant sacrificing some of the complexity and the more difficult aspects of the *Treatise: Essays, Moral* and Political (1741–1742), *Philosophical Essays Concerning Human Understanding* (1748), *An Inquiry Concerning the Principles of Morals* (1751), and *Political Discourses* (1752). He then turned to *The History of England* (1754–1762). The admirable, *Dialogues Concerning Natural Religion* rediscovers once again that great complexity and clarity. It is perhaps the only case of real dialogues in philosophy; there are not two characters, but three, who play many parts, forming temporary alliances, breaking them, becoming reconciled, and so on: Demea, the upholder of revealed religion; Cleanthes, the representative of natural religion; and Philo, the skeptic. Hume-Philo's humor is not simply a way of bringing everyone to agreement in the name of a skepticism that distributes "degrees" but also a way of breaking with the dominant trends of the eighteenth century and of anticipating a philosophy of the future.

CHAPTER THREE

Nietzsche

The Life

The first book of *Thus Spoke Zarathustra* begins with the story of three metamorphoses: "How the spirit becomes camel, the camel becomes lion, and how finally the lion becomes child." The camel is the animal who carries: he carries the weight of established values, the burdens of education, morality, and culture. He carries them into the desert, where he turns into a lion; the lion destroys statues, tramples burdens, and leads the critique of all established values. Finally, the lion must become child, that is, he who represents play and a new beginning — creator of new values and new principles of evaluation.

According to Nietzsche, these three metamorphoses designate, among other things, the different moments of his work, as well as the stages of his life and health. These divisions are no doubt arbitrary: the lion is present in the camel; the child is in the lion; and in the child, there is already the tragic outcome.

Friedrich Wilhelm Nietzsche was born in 1844, in the presbytery of Röcken, in a region of Thuringia that was annexed by Prussia. Both sides of his family came from Lutheran priests. His father, delicate and well educated, himself also a priest, died in 1849 of a softening of the brain (encephalitis or apoplexy). Nietzsche was brought up in Naumburg, surrounded by women, with his younger sister, Elisabeth. He was a child prodigy; his essays were saved, as well as his attempts at musical composition. He studied in Pforta, then in Bonn and Leipzig. He chose philology over theology. But he was already haunted by philosophy and by the image of Arthur Schopenhauer, the solitary thinker, the "private thinker." As early as 1869, Nietzsche's philological works (on Theognis, Simonides, Diogenes Laertius) secured him a professorship in philology at the University of Basel.

It was then that his close friendship with Richard Wagner began. They met in Leipzig. Wagner lived in Tribschen, near Lucerne. Nietzsche said those days were among the best of his life. Wagner was almost sixty; his wife, Cosima, just past thirty. Cosima was Liszt's daughter. She left the musician Hans von Bülow for Wagner. Her friends sometimes called her Ariadne and suggested the parallelisms: Bülow-Theseus, Wagner-Dionysus. Nietzsche encountered here an affective structure that he had already sensed was his and that he would make more and more his own. But these glorious days were not trouble-free: sometimes he had the unpleasant feeling that Wagner was using him and borrowing his own concept of the tragic; sometimes he had the delightful feeling that with Cosima's help he would carry Wagner to truths that he, Wagner, couldn't discover on his own.

Nietzsche's professorship made him a Swiss citizen. He worked as an ambulance driver during the war of 1870. At Basel, he shed his last "burdens": a certain nationalism and a certain sympathy for Bismarck and Prussia. He could no longer stand the identification of culture with the state, nor could he accept the idea that victory through arms be taken as a sign of culture. His disdain for Germany was already apparent, as well as his incapacity for living among the Germans. But with Nietzsche, the abandonment of old beliefs did not assume the form of crisis (what occasioned a crisis was rather the inspiration or the revelation of a new idea). Abandonment was not his problem. We have no reason to suspect his declarations in *Ecce Homo* when he says that in religious matters, despite his ancestry, atheism came to him naturally, instinctively.

Nietzsche retreated further into solitude. In 1871, he wrote *The Birth of Tragedy*, where the real Nietzsche breaks through from behind the masks of Wagner and Schopenhauer. The book was poorly received by philologists. Nietzsche felt himself to be untimely and discovered the incompatibility between the private thinker and the public professor. In the fourth volume of *Untimely Meditations,* "Richard Wagner in Bayreuth" (1875), his reservations about Wagner become explicit. The Bayreuth inauguration, with its circus-like atmosphere, its processions, its speeches, the presence of the old emperor, made him sick. The apparent changes in Nietzsche astonished his friends. He was more and more interested in the sciences: in physics, biology, medicine. His health was poor; he had constant headaches, stomachaches, eye trouble, speech difficulties. He gave up teaching. "My illness slowly liberated me: it spared me separations, violent or ugly actions. . . . It entitled me to radically change my ways." And since Wagner was a compensation for Nietzsche-the-Professor, when the professorship went, so did Wagner.

Thanks to Franz Overbeck, the most loyal and intelligent of his friends, Nietzsche obtained a pension from Basel in 1878. It was then that his itinerant life began: like a shadow, renting simple furnished rooms, seeking favorable climates, he went from resort to resort, in Switzerland, in Italy, in the south of France, sometimes alone, sometimes with friends (Malwida von Meysenbug, an old Wagnerian; his former student Peter Gast, a musician he hoped would replace Wagner; Paul Rée, with whom he shared a taste for the natural sciences and the dissection of morality). He sometimes returned to Naumburg. In Sorrento, he saw Wagner for the last time, a Wagner who had become pious and nationalistic. In 1878, with *Human, All Too Human*, he began his great critique of values, the age of the lion. His friends misunderstood him; Wagner attacked him. But above all, he was increasingly ill. "Not to be able to read! To write only very infrequently! To see no one! Not to hear any music!" In 1880, he described his state as follows: "Continual suffering, for hours every day a feeling of seasickness, a semi-paralysis that makes speaking difficult and, as a diversion, terrible attacks (during the last one I vomited for three days and three nights, and hungered for death...). If I could only describe the relentlessness of it all, the continuous gnawing pain in my head, my eyes, and this general feeling of paralysis, from head to toe."

In what sense is illness — or even madness — present in Nietzsche's work? It is never a source of inspiration. Never did Nietzsche think of philosophy as

proceeding from suffering or anguish, even if the philosopher, according to him, suffers in excess. Nor did
he think of illness as an event that affects a body-
object or a brain-object from the outside. Rather, he
saw in illness a *point of view* on health; and in health, a
point of view on illness. "To observe, as a sick person,
healthier concepts, healthier values, then, conversely,
from the height of a rich, abundant, and confident life,
to delve into the secret work of decadent instincts —
such is the practice in which I most frequently engaged...." Illness is not a motive for a thinking subject, nor is it an object for thought: it constitutes,
rather, a secret intersubjectivity at the heart of a single
individual. Illness as an evaluation of health, health as
an evaluation of illness: such is the "reversal," the "*shift
in perspective*" that Nietzsche saw as the crux of his
method and his calling for a transmutation of values.[1]
Despite appearances, however, there is no reciprocity
between the two points of view, the two evaluations.
Thus movement from health to sickness, from sickness to health, if only as an idea, this very mobility is
the sign of superior health; this mobility, this lightness in movement, is the sign of "great health." That is
why Nietzsche could say until the end (that is, in 1888):
"I am the opposite of a sick person; I am basically
well." And yet one must say that it would all end badly,

for the mad Nietzsche is precisely the Nietzsche who lost this mobility, this art of displacement, when he could no longer *in his health* make of sickness a point of view on health.

With Nietzsche, everything is mask. His health was a first mask for his genius; his suffering, a second mask, both for his genius and for his health. Nietzsche didn't believe in the unity of a self and didn't experience it. Subtle relations of power and of evaluation between different "selves" that conceal but also express other kinds of forces — forces of life, forces of thought — such is Nietzsche's conception, his way of living. Wagner, Schopenhauer, and even Paul Rée were experienced as his own masks. After 1890, his friends (Overbeck, Gast) sometimes thought his madness was his final mask. He had written: "And sometimes madness itself is the mask that hides a knowledge that is fatal and too sure." In fact, it is not. Rather, it marks the moment when the masks, no longer shifting and communicating, merge into a death-like rigidity. Among the strongest moments of Nietzsche's philosophy are the pages where he speaks of the need to be masked, of the virtue and the positivity of masks, of their ultimate importance. Nietzsche's own beauty resided in his hands, his ears, his eyes (he compliments himself on his ears; he sees small ears as being a labyrinthine secret that leads to Dionysus). But on this first mask there comes another, represented by the enormous mustache: "Give me, please give me... — What? — another mask, a second mask."

After *Human, All Too Human*, Nietzsche continued his project of total criticism: *The Wanderer and His Shadow* (1879), *Daybreak* (1880). He worked on *The Gay Science*. But something new emerged: an exaltation, an overabundance, as if Nietzsche had been pushed to the point where evaluation changes meaning and where illness is judged from the height of a strange well-being. His suffering continued, but it was often dominated by an "enthusiasm" that affected his very body. Nietzsche then experienced his most exalted states of being, though they were interlaced with menacing feelings. In August 1881, in Sils-Maria, as he walked along the lake of Silvaplana, he had the overwhelming revelation of the eternal return, then the inspiration for *Thus Spoke Zarathustra*. Between 1883 and 1885, he wrote the four books of *Zarathustra* and gathered notes for a book that was to follow. He carried criticism to a higher level than ever before; he made of it the weapon of a "transmutation" of values, the No that is at the service of a higher affirmation (*Beyond Good and Evil*, 1886; *The Genealogy of Morals*, 1887). This is the third metamorphosis, or the becoming-child.

But he was often very anxious and experienced many frustrations. In 1882, there was the affair with Lou von Salomé, a young Russian woman who lived with Paul Rée and seemed to Nietzsche an ideal disciple and worthy of his love. Following an affective structure he had already had occasion to enact, Nietzsche soon proposed to her through a friend. He was pursuing a dream: with himself as Dionysus, he would receive Ariadne, with Theseus's approval. Theseus is the higher man, the image of the father — what Wagner had already been for Nietzsche. But Nietzsche had not dared to aspire openly to Cosima-Ariadne. In Paul Rée, and in other friends before him, Nietzsche found other Theseuses, fathers that were younger, less imposing.[2] Dionysus is superior to the higher man, as Nietzsche was to Wagner and all the more so to Paul Rée. Obviously and inevitably, this sort of fantasy had to fail. Ariadne always still prefers Theseus. With Malwida von Meysenbug acting as chaperon, Lou von Salomé, Paul Rée, and Nietzsche formed a peculiar quartet. Their life together was made of quarrels and reconciliations. Nietzsche's sister Elisabeth, who was possessive and jealous, did her best to break it up. She succeeded, because Nietzsche could neither detach himself from her nor dampen the harsh judgment he had of her ("people like my sister are irreconcilable adversaries of my way of thinking and my philosophy, this is due to the eternal nature of things..."; "souls such as yours, my poor sister, I do not like them"; "I am profoundly tired of your indecent moralizing chatter..."). Lou von Salomé's fondness for Nietzsche was not truly love; but many years later, she did write a beautiful book about him.[3]

Nietzsche felt more and more isolated. He learned of Wagner's death, which revived in him the Ariadne-Cosima idea. In 1885, Elisabeth married Bernhard Förster, a Wagnerian and an anti-Semite who was also a Prussian nationalist. Förster went to Paraguay with Elisabeth to found a colony of pure Aryans. Nietzsche didn't attend their wedding and found his cumbersome brother-in-law hard to put up with. To another racist he wrote: "Please stop sending me your publications; I fear for my patience." Nietzsche's bouts of euphoria and depression followed more closely on each other. At times, everything seemed excellent to him: his clothes, what he ate, the people who received him, the fascination he believed he caused in stores. At other times, despair won over: a lack of readers, a feeling of death, of deceit.

Then came the great year 1888: *Twilight of the Idols, The Wagner Case, The Antichrist, Ecce Homo.* It is as if his creative faculties were becoming exacerbated in a last momentum before the final collapse. Even his tone changes in these masterful works: a new violence, a new humor, as with the comedy of the Overman. Nietzsche paints a picture of himself that is global, provoking ("one day the memory of something extraordinary will be linked to my name"; "it is only thanks to me that there are great politics on earth"); but at the same time, he focused on the present and was concerned with immediate success. By the end of 1888, he had started to write strange letters. To August Strindberg: "I convened in Rome an assembly of princes, I want to have the young Kaiser shot. Good-bye for now! For we will meet again. On one condition: Let's divorce... Nietzsche-Caesar." On January 3, 1889, he had a crisis in Turin. He again wrote letters, signed them Dionysus, or the Crucified one, or both. To Cosima Wagner: "Ariadne, I love you. Dionysius." Overbeck rushed to Turin, where he found Nietzsche overwrought and lost. He managed to take him to Basel, where Nietzsche calmly allowed himself to be committed. The diagnosis was "progressive paralysis." His mother had him transferred to Jena. The doctors in Jena suspected a syphilitic infection dating back to 1866. (Was this based on some declaration of Nietzsche's? As a young man, he told his friend Paul Deussen of a strange adventure in which he was saved by a piano. A text of

Zarathustra, "Among the Girls of the Desert," must be read in this light.) Sometimes calm, sometimes in crisis, he seemed to have forgotten everything about his work, though he still played music. His mother took him back to her home; Elisabeth returned from Paraguay at the end of 1890. His illness slowly progressed toward total apathy and agony. He died in Weimar in 1900.[4]

Though we cannot know for certain, the diagnosis of an overall paralysis seems accurate. But the question is: Did the symptoms of 1875, 1881, 1888 constitute one and the same clinical picture? Was it the same illness? It seems likely. Whether it was dementia rather than psychosis isn't significant. We have seen in what way illness, and even madness, figured in Nietzsche's work. The overall paralysis marks the moment when illness exits from the work, interrupts it, and makes its continuation impossible. Nietzsche's last letters testify to this extreme moment, thus they still belong to his work; they are a part of it. As long as Nietzsche could practice the art of shifting perspectives, from health to illness and back, he enjoyed, sick as he may have been, the "great health" that made his work possible. But when this art failed him, when the masks were conflated into that of a dunce and a buffoon under the effect of some organic process, the illness

itself became inseparable from the end of his oeuvre
(Nietzsche had spoken of madness as a "comic solu-
tion," as a final farce).

Elisabeth helped her mother take care of Nietzsche.
She gave pious interpretations to the illness. She made
acid remarks to Overbeck, who responded with much
dignity. She had great merits: she did everything to
ensure the diffusion of her brother's ideas; she orga-
nized the Nietzsche-Archiv in Weimar.[5] But these
merits pale before the highest treason: she tried to
place Nietzsche in the service of national socialism.
This was the last stroke of Nietzsche's fate: the abu-
sive family member who figures in the procession of
every "*cursed thinker.*"

The Philosophy

Nietzsche introduced two forms of expression into
philosophy: aphorism and poetry. They imply a new
conception of philosophy, a new image of the thinker
and of thought. Nietzsche replaced the ideal of knowledge, the discovery of the truth, with *interpretation*
and *evaluation*. Interpretation establishes the "meaning" of a phenomenon, which is always fragmentary
and incomplete; evaluation determines the hierarchi-
cal "value" of the meanings and totalizes the fragments
without diminishing or eliminating their plurality.

Indeed, aphorism is both the art of interpreting and what must be interpreted; poetry, both the art of evaluating and what must be evaluated. The interpreter is the physiologist or doctor, the one who sees phenomena as symptoms and speaks through aphorisms. The evaluator is the artist who considers and creates "perspectives" and speaks through poetry. The philosopher of the future is both artist and doctor — in one word, legislator.

This image of the philosopher is also the oldest, the most ancient one. It is that of the pre-Socratic thinker, "physiologist" and artist, interpreter and evaluator of the world. How are we to understand this closeness between the future and the past? The philosopher of the future is the explorer of ancient worlds, of peaks and caves, who creates only inasmuch as he recalls something that has been essentially forgotten. That something, according to Nietzsche, is the unity of life and thought. It is a complex unity: one step for life, one step for thought. Modes of life inspire ways of thinking; modes of thinking create ways of living. Life *activates* thought, and thought in turn *affirms* life. Of this pre-Socratic unity we no longer have even the slightest idea. We now have only instances where thought bridles and mutilates life, making it sensible, and where life takes revenge and drives thought mad,

66

losing itself along the way. Now we only have the choice between mediocre lives and mad thinkers. Lives that are too docile for thinkers, and thoughts too mad for the living: Immanuel Kant and Friedrich Hölderlin. But the fine unity in which madness would cease to be such is yet to be rediscovered — a unity that turns an anecdote of life into an aphorism of thought, and an evaluation of thought into a new perspective on life.

In a way, this secret of the pre-Socratics was already lost at the start. We must think of philosophy as a force. But the law of forces is such that they can only appear when concealed by the mask of preexisting forces. Life must first imitate matter. It was for this reason that to survive at the time of its birth in Greece, philosophical force had to disguise itself. The philosopher had to assume the air of the preceding forces; he had to take on the mask of the *priest*. The young Greek philosopher has something of the old Oriental priest. We still confuse them today: Zoroaster and Heraclitus, the Hindus and the Eleatics, the Egyptians and Empedocles, Pythagoras and the Chinese. We speak of the virtue of the ideal philosopher, of his asceticism, of his love of wisdom. We cannot guess the peculiar solitude and the sensuality, the very unwise ends of the perilous existence that lie beneath this mask. The secret of philosophy, because it was lost at the start, remains to be discovered in the future.

It was therefore fated that philosophy degenerate as it developed through history, that it turn against itself and be taken in by its own mask. Instead of linking an active life and an affirmative thinking, thought gives itself the task of judging life, opposing to it supposedly higher values, measuring it against these values, restricting and condemning it. And at the same time that thought thus becomes negative, life depreciates, ceases to be active, is reduced to its weakest forms, to sickly forms that are alone compatible with the so-called higher values. *It is the triumph of "reaction" over active life and of negation over affirmative thought.* The consequences for philosophy are dire, for the virtues of the philosopher as legislator were first the critique of all established values — that is, of values superior to life and of the principles on which they depend — and then the creation of new values, of values of life that call for another principle. Hammer and transmutation. While philosophy thus degenerates, the philosopher as legislator is replaced by the submissive philosopher. Instead of the critic of established values, instead of the creator of new values and new evaluations, there emerges the preserver of accepted values. The philosopher ceases to be a physiologist or doctor and becomes a metaphysician. He ceases to be a poet and becomes a "public professor." He claims to be beholden to the requirements of truth and reason; but beneath these requirements of reason are forces that aren't so reasonable at all: the state, religion, all the current values. Philosophy becomes nothing more than taking the census of all the reasons man gives himself to obey. The philosopher invokes love of the truth, but it is a truth that harms no one ("it appears as a self-contented and happy creature which is continually assuring all the powers that be that no one needs to be the least concerned on its account; for it is, after all, only "pure science").[6] The philosopher evaluates life in accordance with his ability to uphold weights and carry burdens. These burdens, these weights, are precisely the higher values. Such is the spirit of heaviness that brings together, in the same desert, the carrier with the carried, the reactive and depreciated life with negative and depreciating thinking. All that remains then is an illusion of critique and a phantom of creation, for nothing is more opposed to the creator than the carrier. To create is to lighten, to unburden life, to invent new possibilities of life. The creator is legislator — dancer.

The degeneration of philosophy appears clearly with Socrates. If we define metaphysics by the dis-

tinction between two worlds, by the opposition between essence and appearance, between the true and
the false, the intelligible and the sensible, we have to
say that it is Socrates who invented metaphysics. He
made of life something that must be judged, measured,
restricted, and of thought, a measure, a limit, that is
exercised in the name of higher values: the Divine,
the True, the Beautiful, the Good.... With Socrates
emerges the figure of a philosopher who is voluntar-
ily and subtly submissive. But let's move on and skip
through the centuries. Who can really think that Kant
reinstated critique or rediscovered the idea of the philosopher as legislator? Kant denounces false claims to
knowledge, but he doesn't question the ideal of knowing; he denounces false morality, but he doesn't question the claims of morality or the nature and the origin
of its value. He blames us for having confused domains
and interests; but the domains remain intact, and the
interests of reason, sacred (true knowledge, true morals,
true religion).

Dialectics itself perpetrates this prestigiditation.
Dialectics is the art that invites us to recuperate alien-
ated properties. Everything returns to the Spirit as
the motor and product of the dialectic, or to self-con-
sciousness, or even to man, as generic being. But if
our properties in themselves express a diminished life

and a mutilating thought, what is the use of recuperating them or becoming their true subject? Did we do
away with religion when we interiorized the priest,
placing him into the faithful, in the style of the Reformation? Did we kill God when we put man in his
place and kept the most important thing, which is the
place? The only change is this: instead of being bur-
dened from the outside, man takes the weights and
places them on his own back. The philosopher of the
future, the doctor-philosopher, will diagnose the per-
petuation of the same ailment beneath different symptoms; values can change, man can put himself in the
place of God, progress, happiness; utility can replace
the truth, the good, or the divine — what is essential
hasn't changed: the perspectives or the evaluations on
which these values, whether old or new, depend. We
are always asked to submit ourselves, to burden ourselves, to recognize only the reactive forms of life, the
accusatory forms of thought. When we no longer want,
when we can no longer bear higher values, we are
still asked to accept "the real as it is" — but *this "real as
it is" is precisely what the higher values have made of
reality*! (Even existentialism retained a frightening
taste for carrying, for bearing, a properly dialectical
taste that separates it from Nietzsche.)

Nietzsche is the first to tell us that killing God is

not enough to bring about the transmutation of values. In his work, there are at least fifteen versions of
the death of God, all of them very beautiful.[7] But
indeed, in one of the most beautiful, the murderer of
God is "the ugliest of men." What Nietzsche means is
that man makes himself even more ugly when, no
longer in need of an external authority, he denies
himself what was denied him and spontaneously takes
on the policing and the burdens that he no longer
thinks come from the outside. Thus the history of
philosophy, from the Socratics to the Hegelians, remains the long history of man's submissions and the
reasons he gives himself for legitimizing them. This
process of degeneration concerns not only philosophy but also becoming in general, or the most basic
category of history — not a fact in history, but the very
principle from which derive most of the events that
have determined our thinking and our life, the symptoms of a decomposition. And so true philosophy, as
philosophy of the future, is no more historical than it
is eternal: it must be untimely, always untimely.

All interpretations determine the meaning of a
phenomenon. Meaning consists of a relation of forces
in which some *act* and others *react* in a complex and
hierarchized whole. Whatever the complexity of a
phenomenon, we can distinguish primary forces, of

conquest and subjugation, from reactive, secondary forces, of adaptation and regulation. This distinction is not only quantitative but also qualitative and typological, for it is in the nature of forces to be in relation to other forces and it is in this relation that they acquire their essence or quality. The relation of force to force is called "will." That is why we must avoid at all costs the misinterpretations of the Nietzschean principle of the will to power. This principle doesn't mean (or at least doesn't primarily mean) that the will *wants* power or *wishes* to dominate. As long as the will to power is interpreted in terms of a "desire to dominate," we inevitably make it depend on established values, the only ones able to determine, in any given case or conflict, who must be "recognized" as the most powerful. We then cannot recognize the nature of the will to power as an elastic principle of all of our evaluations, as a hidden principle for the creation of new values not yet recognized. The will to power, says Nietzsche, consists not in coveting or even in *taking* but in *creating* and *giving*. Power, as a will to power, is not that which the will wants, but *that which wants* in the will (Dionysus himself). The will to power is the differential element from which derive the forces at work, as well as their respective quality in a complex whole. Thus it is always given

73

as a mobile, aerial, pluralist element. It is by the will to power that a force commands, but it is also by the will to power that a force obeys. To these two types or qualities of forces there correspond two faces, two qualia, of the will to power, which are ultimate and fluent, deeper than the forces that derive from them, for the will to power makes it that active forces *affirm*, and affirm their difference: in them affirmation is first, and negation is never but a consequence, a sort of surplus of pleasure. What characterizes reactive forces, on the other hand, is their opposition to what they are not, their tendency to limit the other: in them, *negation* comes first; through negation, they arrive at a semblance of affirmation. Affirmation and negation are thus the qualia of the will to power, just as action and reaction are the qualities of forces. And just as interpretation finds the principles of meaning in forces, evaluation finds the principles of values in the will to power. Given the preceding terminological precisions, we can avoid reducing Nietzsche's thought to a simple dualism, for, as we shall see, affirmation is itself essentially multiple and pluralist, whereas negation is always one, or heavily monist.

Yet history presents us with a most peculiar phenomenon: the reactive forces triumph; negation wins in the will to power! This is the case not only in the

74

history of man, but in the history of life and the earth, at least on the face of it inhabited by man. Everywhere we see the victory of No over Yes, of reaction over action. Life becomes adaptive and regulative, reduced to its secondary forms; we no longer understand what it means to act. Even the forces of the earth become exhausted on this desolate face. Nietzsche calls this joint victory of reactive forces and the will to negate "nihilism" — or the triumph of the slaves. According to him, the analysis of nihilism is the object of *psychology*, understood also as a psychology of the cosmos.

It seems difficult for a philosophy of force or of the will to explain how the reactive forces, how the slaves, or the weak, can win. If all that happens is that together they form a force greater than that of the strong, it is hard to see what has changed and what a qualitative evaluation is based on. But in fact, the weak, the slaves, triumph not by adding up their forces but by subtracting those of the other: they separate the strong from what they can do. They triumph not because of the composition of their power but because of the power of their contagion. They bring about a becoming-reactive of all forces. That is what "degeneration" means. Nietzsche shows early on that the criteria of the struggle for life, of natural selection, necessarily favor the weak and the sick, the "secondary ones" (by sick is meant a life reduced to its reactive processes). This is all the more true in the case of man, where the criteria of history favor the slaves as such. It is a becoming-sick of all life, a becoming-slave of all men, that constitutes the victory of nihilism. We must again avoid misconceptions about the Nietzschean terms "strong" and "weak," "master" and "slave": it is clear that the slave doesn't stop being a slave when he gets power, nor do the weak cease to be weak. Even when they win, reactive forces are still reactive. In everything, according to Nietzsche, what is at stake is a qualitative typology: a question of baseness and nobility. Our masters are slaves that have triumphed in a universal becoming-slave: European man, domesticated man, the buffoon. Nietzsche describes modern states as ant colonies, where the leaders and the powerful win through their baseness, through the contagion of this baseness and this buffoonery. Whatever the complexity of Nietzsche's work, the reader can easily guess in which category (that is, in which type) he would have placed the race of "masters" conceived by the Nazis. When nihilism triumphs, then and only then does the will to power stop meaning "to create" and start to signify instead "to want power," "to want to dominate" (thus to attribute to oneself or have others attribute to one established values: money, honors, power, and so on). Yet that kind of will to power is precisely that of the slave; it is the way in which the slave or the impotent conceives of power, the idea he has of it and that *he applies when he triumphs*. It can happen that a sick person says, Oh! if I were well, I would do this or that — and maybe he will, but his plans and his thoughts are still those of a sick person, only a sick person. The same goes for the slave and for his conception of mastery or power. The same also goes for the reactive man and his conception of action. Values and evaluations are always being reversed, things are always seen from a petty angle, images are reversed as in a bull's-eye. One of Nietzsche's greatest sayings is: "We must always protect the strong from the weak."

Let us now specify, for the case of man, the stages of the triumph of nihilism. These stages constitute the great discoveries of Nietzschean psychology, the categories of a typology of depths.

1. *Resentment*: It's your fault... It's your fault... Projective accusation and recrimination. It's your fault if I'm weak and unhappy. Reactive life gets away from active forces; reaction stops being "acted." It becomes something sensed, a "resentment" that is exerted against everything that is active. Action becomes

77

shameful: life itself is accused, separated from its power, separated from what it can do. The lamb says: I could do everything that the eagle does; I'm admirable for not doing so. Let the eagle do as I do...

2. *Bad conscience*: It's my fault... The moment of introjection. Having captured life like a fish on a hook, the reactive forces can turn in on themselves. They interiorize the fault, say they are guilty, turn against themselves. But in this way they set an example, they invite all of life to come and join them, they acquire a maximum of contagious power — they form reactive communities.

3. *The ascetic ideal*: The moment of sublimation. What the weak or reactive life ultimately wants is the negation of life. *Its* will to power is a will to nothingness, as a condition of its triumph. Conversely, the will to nothingness can only tolerate a life that is weak, mutilated, reactive — states close to nothing. Then is formed the disturbing alliance. Life is judged according to values that are said to be superior to life: these pious values are opposed to life, condemn it, lead it to nothingness; they promise salvation only to the most reactive, the weakest, the sickest forms of life. Such is the alliance between God-Nothingness and Reactive-Man. Everything is reversed: slaves are called masters; the weak are called strong; baseness is

called nobility. We say that someone is noble and strong because he carries; he carries the weight of higher values; he feels responsible. Even life, especially life, seems hard for him to carry. Evaluations are so distorted that we can no longer see that the carrier is a slave, that what he carries is a slavery, that the carrier is a carrier of the weak — the opposite of a creator or a dancer. In fact, one only carries out of weakness; one only wishes to be carried out of a will to nothingness (see the buffoon of *Zarathustra* and the figure of the donkey).

These stages of nihilism correspond, according to Nietzsche, to Judaic religion, then to Christianity, but the latter was certainly well prepared by Greek philosophy, that is, by the degeneration of philosophy in Greece. More generally, Nietzsche shows how these stages are also the genesis of the great categories of our thought: the Self, the World, God, causality, finality, and so on. But nihilism doesn't stop there and follows a path that makes up our entire history.

4. *The death of God:* The moment of recuperation. For a long time, the death of God was thought to be an inter-religious drama, a problem between the Jewish God and the Christian God, to the point where we are no longer quite sure whether it is the Son who dies out of resentment against the Father or the

Father who dies so that the Son can be independent (and become "cosmopolitan"). But Saint Paul already founded Christianity on the principle that Christ dies for *our* sins. With the Reformation, the death of God becomes increasingly a problem between God and man, until the day man discovers himself to be the murderer of God, wishes to see himself as such and to carry this new weight. He wants the logical outcome of this death: to become God himself, to replace God.

Nietzsche's idea is that the death of God is a grand event, glamorous yet insufficient, for nihilism continues, barely changing its form. Earlier, nihilism had meant depreciation, the negation of life in the name of higher values. But now the negation of these higher values is replaced by human values — all too human values (morals replace religion; utility, progress, even history replace divine values). Nothing has changed, for the same reactive life, the same slavery that had triumphed in the shadow of divine values now triumphs through human ones. The same carrier, the same donkey, who used to bear the weight of divine relics, for which he answered before God, now burdens himself on his own, as an auto-responsibility. We have even taken a further step in the desert of nihilism: we claim to embrace all of reality, but we embrace only what the higher values have left of it, the residue of reactive forces and the will to nothingness. That is why Nietzsche, in book IV of *Zarathustra*, traces the great misery of those he calls "the higher men." These men want to replace God; they carry human values; they even believe they are rediscovering reality, recuperating the meaning of affirmation. But the only affirmation of which they are capable is the Yes of the donkey, Y-A, the reactive force that burdens itself with the products of nihilism and that thinks it says Yes each time it *carries* a no. (Two modern works are profound meditations on the Yes and the No, on their authenticity or their mystification: those of Nietzsche and James Joyce.)

5. *The last man and the man who wants to die*: The moment of the end. The death of God is thus an event that still awaits its meaning and its value. As long as our principle of evaluation remains unchanged, as long as we replace old values with new ones that only amount to new combinations between reactive forces and the will to nothingness, nothing has changed; we are still under the aegis of *established* values. We know full well that some values are born old and from the time of their birth exhibit their conformity, their conformism, their inability to upset any established order. And yet with each step, nihilism advances further, inanity further reveals itself. What appears in the death

of God is that the alliance between reactive forces and the will to nothingness, between reactive man and nihilist God, is in the process of dissolving: man claimed he could do without God, be the same as God. Nietzsche's concepts are categories of the unconscious. What counts is how this drama is played out in the unconscious: when reactive forces claim to do without a "will," they fall further and further into the abyss of nothingness, into a world more and more devoid of values, divine or even human. Following the higher men there arises *the last man*, the one who says: all is vain, better to fade away passively! Better a nothingness of the will than a will of nothingness! But thanks to this rupture, the will to nothingness turns against the reactive forces, becomes the will to deny reactive life itself, and inspires in man the wish to actively destroy himself. Beyond the last man, then, there is still *the man who wants to die*. And at this moment of the completion of nihilism (midnight), everything is ready — ready for a transmutation.[8]

The transmutation of all values is defined in the following way: an active becoming of forces, *a triumph of affirmation in the will to power*. Under the rule of nihilism, negation is the form and the content of the will to power; affirmation is only secondary, subordinated to negation, gathering and carrying its fruit.

Hence the Yes of the donkey, Y-A, becomes a false yes, a sort of caricature of affirmation. Now everything changes: affirmation becomes the essence or the will to power itself; as for the negative, it subsists, but as the mode of being of one who affirms, as the aggressivity that belongs to affirmation, like the lightning that announces and the thunder that follows, what is affirmed — like the total critique that accompanies creation. Thus Zarathustra is pure affirmation but also he who carries negation to its highest point, making of it an action, an agency that services he who affirms and creates. The Yes of Zarathustra is opposed to the Yes of the donkey, as creating is opposed to carrying. The No of Zarathustra is opposed to the No of nihilism, as aggressivity is opposed to resentment. Transmutation signifies this reversal in the relation of affirmation-negation. But we can see that a transmutation is possible only at the close of nihilism. We had to get to the last man, then to the man who wants to die, for negation *finally to turn against the reactive forces* and become an action that serves a higher affirmation (hence Nietzsche's saying: nihilism conquered, but conquered by itself...).

Affirmation is the highest power of the will. But what is affirmed? The earth, life... But what form do the earth and life assume when they are the objects of affirmation? A form unbeknownst to we who inhabit only the desolate surface of the earth and who live in states close to zero. What nihilism condemns and tries to deny is not so much Being, for we have known for some time that Being resembles Nothingness like a brother. It is, rather, multiplicity; it is, rather, becoming. Nihilism considers becoming as something that *must* atone and must be reabsorbed into Being, and the multiple as something unjust that must be judged and reabsorbed into the One. Becoming and multiplicity are guilty — such is the first and the last word of nihilism. That is why under its aegis, philosophy is motivated by dark sentiments: a "discontent," a certain anguish, an uneasiness about living, an obscure sense of guilt. By contrast, the first figure of the transmutation elevates multiplicity and becoming to their highest power and makes of them objects of an affirmation. In the affirmation of the multiple lies the practical joy of the diverse. Joy emerges as the sole motive for philosophizing. To valorize negative sentiments or sad passions — that is the mystification on which nihilism bases its power. (Lucretius, then Spinoza, already wrote decisive passages on this subject. Before Nietzsche, they conceived philosophy as the power to affirm, as the practical struggle against mystifications, as the expulsion of the negative.)

Multiplicity is affirmed as multiplicity; becoming is affirmed as becoming. That is to say at once that affirmation is itself multiple, that it becomes itself, and that becoming and multiplicity are themselves affirmations. There is something like a play of mirrors in affirmation properly understood: "Eternal affirmation...eternally I am your affirmation!" The second figure of the transmutation is the affirmation of the affirmation, the doubling, the divine couple Dionysus and Ariadne.

Dionysus can be recognized in all the preceding characteristics. We are far from the first Dionysus, the one that Nietzsche had conceived under the influence of Schopenhauer, who had reabsorbed life into a primal ground and, forming an alliance with Apollo, had created tragedy. It is true that starting with *The Birth of Tragedy,* Dionysus was defined through his opposition to Socrates even more than through his alliance with Apollo; Socrates judged and condemned life in the name of higher values, but Dionysus had the sense that life is not to be judged, that it is just enough, holy enough, in itself. And as Nietzsche progresses further in his work, the real opposition appears to him: no longer Dionysus versus Socrates, but Dionysus versus the Crucified. Their martyrdom seems the same, but the interpretation, the evaluation of it are different: on one side, a testimony against life, a vengeance that consists in denying life; on the other, the affirmation of life, the affirmation of becoming and multiplicity that extends even in the very laceration and scattered limbs of Dionysus. Dance, lightness, laughter are the properties of Dionysus. As power of affirmation, Dionysus evokes a mirror within his mirror, a ring within his ring: a second affirmation is needed for affirmation to be itself affirmed. Dionysus has a fiancée, Ariadne ("You have small ears, you have my ears: put a clever word in them"). The only clever word is Yes. Ariadne completes the set of relations that define Dionysus and the Dionysian philosopher.

Multiplicity is no longer answerable to the One, nor is becoming answerable to Being. But Being and the One do more than lose their meaning: they take on a new meaning. Now the One is said of the multiple as the multiple (splinters or fragments); Being is said of becoming as becoming. That is the Nietzschean reversal, or the third figure of the transmutation. Becoming is no longer opposed to Being, nor is the multiple opposed to the One (these oppositions being the categories of nihilism). On the contrary, what is affirmed is the One of multiplicity, the Being of becoming. Or, as Nietzsche puts it, one affirms the necessity of chance. Dionysus is a player. The real player makes of chance an object of affirmation: he affirms the fragments, the elements of chance; from this affirmation is born the necessary number, which brings back the throw of the dice. We now see what this third figure is: the play of the eternal return. This return is precisely the Being of becoming, the one of multiplicity, the necessity of chance. Thus we must not make of the eternal return a *return of the same*. To do this would be to misunderstand the form of the transmutation and the change in the fundamental re-lationship, for the same does not preexist the diverse (except in the category of nihilism). *It is not the same that comes back*, since the coming back is the original form of the same, which is said only of the diverse, the multiple, becoming. The same doesn't come back; only coming back is the same in what becomes.

The very essence of the eternal return is at issue. We must get rid of all sorts of useless themes in this question of the eternal return. It is sometimes asked how Nietzsche could have believed this thought to be new or extraordinary, because it was quite common among the ancients. But, precisely, Nietzsche knew full well that *it was not to be found* in ancient philoso-phy, either in Greece or in the Orient, except in a piecemeal or hesitant manner and in a very different sense from his own. Nietzsche already had the most explicit reservations about Heraclitus. And in putting the eternal return in the mouth of Zarathustra, like a serpent in the gullet, Nietzsche meant only to impute to the ancient figure of Zoroaster what Zoroaster himself was the least able to conceive. Nietzsche explains that he takes Zarathustra as a euphemism, or rather as an antithesis and a metonymy, purposely giving him new concepts that he himself could not create.[9]

It is also asked why the eternal return is so surprising if it consists of a cycle, that is, of a return of the whole, a return of the same, a return to the same. But in fact it is not that at all. Nietzsche's secret is that *the eternal return is selective.* And doubly so. First as a thought, for it gives us a law for the autonomy of the will freed from any morality: whatever I want (my laziness, my gluttony, my cowardice, my vice as well as my virtue), I "must" want it in such a way that I also want its eternal return. The world of "semi-wants" is thus eliminated: everything we want when we say "once, only once." Even a cowardice, a laziness, that would wish for its eternal return would become something other than a laziness, a cowardice; it would become an active power of affirmation.

The eternal return is not only selective thinking but also selective Being. Only affirmation comes back, only what can be affirmed comes back, only joy returns. All that can be negated, all that is negation, is expelled by the very movement of the eternal return. We may fear that the combination of nihilism and reaction will eternally come back. The eternal return should be compared to a wheel whose movement is endowed with a centrifugal force that drives out everything negative. Because Being is affirmed of becoming, it expels all that contradicts affirmation, all the forms of nihilism and of reaction: bad conscience, resentment . . . we will see them only once.

Yet in many texts, Nietzsche conceives of the eternal return as a cycle where everything comes back, or the same comes back, which amounts to the same. But what do these texts mean? Nietzsche is a thinker who "dramatizes" ideas, that is, who presents them as successive events, with different levels of tension. We have already seen this with the death of God. Similarly, the eternal return is the object of two accounts (and there would have been more had his work not been interrupted by madness, which prevented a progression that Nietzsche had explicitly planned). Of the two accounts, one concerns a *sick* Zarathustra, the other, a Zarathustra who is *convalescent and nearly cured*. What makes Zarathustra sick is precisely the idea of the cycle: the idea that everything comes back, that the same returns, that everything comes back to the same. In this case, the eternal return is only a hypothesis, a hypothesis that is both banal and terrifying: banal because it corresponds to a natural, animal, immediate, certitude (that is why, when the eagle and the serpent try to console him, Zarathustra answers: you have made of the eternal return a tired refrain, you have reduced the eternal return to a formula that is common, all too common);[10] terrifying because, if it is true that everything comes back, and comes back to the same, then small and petty man, nihilism and reaction, will come back as well (that is why Zarathustra cries out his great disgust, his great contempt, and declares that he can not, will not, dares not, say the eternal return).

What happened when Zarathustra was convalescent? Did he simply decide to bear what he couldn't bear before? He accepts the eternal return; he grasps its joy. Is this simply a psychological change? Of course not. It is a change in the understanding and the meaning of the eternal return itself. Zarathustra recognizes that while he was sick, he had understood nothing of the eternal: that it is not a cycle, that it is not the return of the same, nor a return to the same; that it is not a simple, natural assumption for the use of animals or a sad moral punishment for the use of men.

Zarathustra understands the equation "eternal return = selective Being." How can reaction and nihilism, how can negation come back, since the eternal return is the Being that is only said of affirmation, and becoming in action? A centrifugal wheel, "supreme constellation of Being, that no wish can attain, that no negation can soil." The eternal return is repetition; but it is the repetition that selects, the repetition that saves. The prodigious secret of a repetition that is liberating and selecting.

The transmutation thus has a fourth, and final, dimension: it implies and produces the Overman. In his human essence, man is a reactive being who combines his forces with nihilism. The eternal return repels and expels him. The transmutation involves an essential, radical conversion that is produced in man but that produces the Overman. The Overman refers specifically to the gathering of all that can be affirmed, the superior form of what is, the figure that represents selective Being, its offspring and subjectivity. He is thus at the intersection of two genealogies. On the one hand, he is produced in man, through the intermediary of the last man and the man who wants to die, but beyond them, through a sort of wrenching apart and transformation of human essence. Yet on the other hand, although he is produced in man, he is not produced by man: he is the fruit of Dionysus and Ariadne. Zarathustra himself follows the first genealogical line; he remains thus inferior to Dionysus, whose prophet or herald he becomes. Zarathustra calls the Overman his child, but he has been surpassed by his child, whose real father is Dionysus. Thus the figures of the transmutation are complete: Dionysus or affirmation; Dionysus-Ariadne, or affirmation doubled; the eternal return, or affirmation redoubled; the Overman, or the figure and the product of the affirmation.

We readers of Nietzsche must avoid four potential misinterpretations: (1) about the will to power (believing that the will to power means "wanting to dominate" or "wanting power"); (2) about the strong and the weak (believing that the most powerful in a social regime are thereby the strong); (3) about the eternal return (believing that it is an old idea, borrowed from the Greeks, the Hindus, the Babylonians...; believing that it is a cycle, or a return of the same, a return to the same); (4) about the last works (believing that they are excessive or disqualified by madness).

Dictionary of the Main Characters in Nietzsche's Work

Eagle and Serpent: They are Zarathustra's animals. The serpent is coiled around the eagle's neck. Both thus represent the eternal return as a ring, a ring within the ring, the engagement of the divine couple Dionysus and Ariadne. But they represent it in an animal way, as an immediate certitude or a natural assumption. (What escapes them is the essence of the eternal return, that is, the fact that it is selective, both as thought and as Being.) Thus they make of the eternal return a "babbling," a "refrain." What's more: the *uncoiled* serpent represents what is intolerable and impossible in the eternal return when it is seen as a natural certitude according to which "everything comes back."

Donkey and Camel: They are beasts of the desert (nihilism). They carry loads to the heart of the desert. The donkey has two flaws: his No is a false no, a no of resentment. And moreover, his Yes (Y-A, Y-A) is a false yes. He thinks that to affirm means *to carry, to burden*. The donkey is primarily a Christian animal: he carries the weight of values said to be "superior to life." After the death of God, he burdens himself, he carries the weight of human values, he purports to deal with "the real as it is": he is thus the new god of the higher men. From beginning to end, the donkey is the caricature of the betrayal of Dionysus's Yes; he affirms, but only the products of nihilism. His long ears are also the opposite of the small, round labyrinthine ears of Dionysus and Ariadne.

Spider (or Tarantula): It is the spirit of revenge or resentment. Its power of contagion is its venom. Its will is a will to punish and to judge. Its weapon is the thread, the thread of morality. It preaches equality (that everyone become like it!).

Ariadne and Theseus: She is the anima. She was loved by Theseus and loved him. But that was just when she held the thread and was a bit of a spider, a cold creature of resentment. Theseus is the hero, a picture of the higher man. He has all the inferiorities of the higher man: to carry, to bear, not to know to unharness, to know nothing of lightness. As long as Ariadne loves Theseus and is loved by him, her femininity remains imprisoned, tied up by the thread. But when Dionysus-the-Bull approaches, she discovers true affirmation and lightness. She becomes an affirmative anima who says Yes to Dionysus. Together they are the couple of the eternal return and give birth to the Overman, for "it is only when the hero abandons his soul that the Overman approaches as in a dream."

The Buffoon (Monkey, Dwarf, or Demon): He is the caricature of Zarathustra. He imitates him, but as heaviness imitates lightness. Thus he represents the worst
danger for Zarathustra: the betrayal of the doctrine.
The buffoon is contemptuous, but out of resentment.
He is the spirit of heaviness. Like Zarathustra, he
claims to go beyond, to overcome. But to overcome
means for him either to be carried (to climb on man's
shoulders, or even on Zarathustra's) or to jump over
him. These represent the two possible misreadings of
the "Overman."

Christ (Saint Paul and Buddha): (1) He represents an
essential moment of nihilism: that of bad conscience,
after Judaic resentment. But it is still the same enterprise of vengeance and animosity toward life, for
Christian love valorizes only the sick and desolate aspects of life. Through his death, Christ seems to become independent of the Jewish God: He becomes
universal and "cosmopolitan." But he has only found a
new way of judging life, of universalizing the con-
demnation of life, by internalizing sin (bad conscience). Christ died for us, for our sins! Such at least is
the interpretation of Saint Paul, and it is the one that
has prevailed in the Church and in our history. Christ's
martyrdom is thus opposed to that of Dionysus: in

the first case, life is judged and must atone; in the second, it is sufficiently just in itself to justify everything. "Dionysus against the Crucified."

(2) But if beneath Paul's interpretation we seek the personal type that is Christ, we can surmise that Christ belongs to nihilism in a very different way. He is kind and joyful, doesn't condemn, is indifferent to guilt of any kind; he wants only to die; he seeks his own death. He is thus well ahead of Saint Paul, for he represents the ultimate stage of nihilism: that of the last man or the man who wants to die — the stage closest to Dionysian transmutation. Christ is "the most interesting of decadents," a sort of Buddha. He enables a transmutation; the synthesis of Dionysus and Christ is now possible: "Dionysus-Crucified."

Dionysus: There are many different aspects of Dionysus — in relation to Apollo, in opposition to Socrates, in contrast with Christ, in complementarity with Ariadne.

The Higher Men: They are multiple but exemplify the same endeavor: after the death of God, to replace divine values with human values. They thus represent the becoming of culture, or the attempt to put man in the place of God. As the principle of evaluation remains the same, as the transmutation has not been effected, they belong fully to nihilism and are closer to Zarathustra's buffoon than to Zarathustra himself. They are "failed," "wasted," and know not how to laugh, to play, to dance. In logical sequence, their parade goes as follows:

1. *The Last Pope*: He knows that God is dead but believes that God suffocated himself, out of pity, because he could no longer stand his love for men. The last pope has become master-less, yet he is not free; he lives on his memories.

2. *The Two Kings*: They represent the movement of the "morality of mores," which seeks to train and form men, to create free men through the most violent and restrictive means. Thus there are two kings: one on the left for the means, one on the right for the ends. But before, as well as after, the death of God, for the means as for the ends, the morality of mores itself degenerates, trains and selects the wrong way, falls in favor of the rabble (triumph of the slaves). The two kings are the ones who bring in the donkey so that the higher men will turn into their new god.

3. *The Ugliest of Men*: He is the one who killed God, for he could no longer tolerate his pity. But he is still the old man, uglier yet: instead of the bad conscience of a god who died for him, he experiences the

bad conscience of a god who died because of him; instead of feeling God's pity, he feels man's pity, the pity of the rabble, which is even more unbearable. He is the one who leads the litany of the donkey and encourages the false Yes.

4. *The Man with the Leech*: He wants to replace divine values, religion, and even morality with knowledge. Knowledge must be scientific, exact, incisive, whether its object be big or small; the exact knowledge of the smallest thing will replace our belief in "grand," vague values. That is why this man gives his arm to the leech and gives himself the task and the ideal of knowing a very small thing: the brain of the leech (without going back to first causes). But the man with the leech doesn't know that knowledge is the leech itself and that it acts as a relay for morality and religion by pursuing the very same goals: cutting up life, mutilating and judging life.

5. *The Voluntary Beggar*: He has given up on knowledge. He believes only in human happiness; he seeks happiness on earth. But human happiness, dull as it may be, cannot be found among the rabble, motivated as it is by resentment and bad conscience. Human happiness can only be found among cows.

6. *The Sorcerer*: He is the man of bad conscience, who persists under the reign of God as well as after

his death. Bad conscience is fundamentally a comedian, an exhibitionist. It plays every role, even that of the atheist, even that of the poet, even that of Ariadne. But it always lies and recriminates. When it says "it's my fault," it wants to incite pity, inspire guilt, even in those who are strong; it wants to shame everything that is alive, to propagate its venom. "Your complaint is a decoy!"

7. *The Wandering Shadow*: It is the enterprise of culture that has sought everywhere to accomplish the same goal (to free men, select and train them): under the reign of God, after his death, in knowledge, in happiness, and so on. Everywhere it has failed, for this goal is itself a shadow. This goal, higher man, is also a failure. It is the shadow of Zarathustra, nothing but his shadow, who follows him everywhere but disappears at the two important moments of the transmutation: noon and midnight.

8. *The Soothsayer*: He says "all is vain." He announces the last stage of nihilism: the moment when man, having measured the vanity of his effort to replace God, preferred not to wish at all rather than to wish for nothing. The soothsayer thus announces *the last man*. Prefiguring the end of nihilism, he goes further than the higher men. But what escapes him is what is beyond even the last man: *the man who wants*

to die, the man who wants his own end. It is with him that nihilism truly comes to an end, defeats itself: transmutation and the Overman are near.

Zarathustra and the Lion: Zarathustra is not Dionysus, but only his prophet. There are two ways of expressing this subordination. One could first say that Zarathustra remains at No, though this No is no longer that of nihilism: it is the sacred No of the Lion. It is the destruction of all established values, divine and human, that constituted nihilism. It is the trans-nihilist No inherent to the transmutation. Thus Zarathustra seems to have completed his task when he sinks his hands into the mane of the Lion. But in truth, Zarathustra doesn't remain at No, even the sacred and transmutative No. He fully participates in Dionysian affirmation; he is already the idea of this affirmation, the idea of Dionysus. Just as Dionysus is engaged to Ariadne in the eternal return, Zarathustra finds his fiancée in the eternal return. Just as Dionysus is the father of the Overman, Zarathustra calls the Overman his child. Nonetheless, Zarathustra is overtaken by his own children and is only the pretender to, not the constitutive element of, the ring of the eternal return. He doesn't so much produce the Overman as ensure this production within man, by creating all the conditions in which man overcomes himself and is overcome and in which the Lion becomes Child.

NOTES

1. "Why I Am So Wise," I, in *Ecce Homo*.

2. In 1876, Nietzsche had proposed to a younger woman through his friend Hugo von Senger, who eventually married her.

3. Lou Andreas-Salomé, *Friedrich Nietzsche* (Vienna: C. Konegen, 1894).

4. About Nietzsche's illness, see Erich Friedrich Podach's *The Madness of Nietzsche* (New York: Putnam, 1931).

5. After 1950, the manuscripts were taken to the former building of the Goethe-Schiller Archiv in Weimar.

6. "Schopenhauer as Educator," vol. 3 of *Untimely Meditations*.

7. "The Madman," *Gay Science*, book III, 125, is sometimes quoted as the first major version of the death of God. This is not the case: in *The Wanderer and His Shadow*, there is a wonderful tale called "The Prisoners." This text resonates mysteriously with Franz Kafka.

8. This distinction between the last man and the man who wants to die is fundamental in Nietzsche's philosophy: in *Zarathustra*, for example, compare the prediction of the soothsayer ("The Soothsayer," book II) with the call of Zarathustra (Prologue, 4 and 5).

9. See "Why I Am a Fatality," 3, in *Ecce Homo*. In fact, it is unlikely that the idea of the eternal return had ever been entertained in the ancient world. Greek thought as a whole was reticent on this theme: see Charles Mugler, *Deux Thèmes de la cosmologie grècque: Devenir cyclique et pluralité des mondes* (Paris: Klincksieck, 1953). Specialists admit that the same is true of Chinese, Indian, Iranian, and Babylonian thought. The opposition between a circular time of the ancients and a linear time of the moderns is facile and incorrect. In all respects, we can, with Nietzsche, consider the eternal return a Nietzschean discovery, though with ancient premises.

10. "The Convalescent," 2, in *Thus Spoke Zarathustra*, book III.

Designed by Bruce Mau with Barr Gilmore and Donald Mak
Typeset by Archetype
Printed and bound by Maple-Vail on Sebago acid-free paper